TIM AND SALLY'S

YEAR IN POEMS

GRADY THRASHER

ILLUSTRATIONS BY ELAINE HEARN RABON

JONQUIL BOOKS ❧ ATHENS, GEORGIA

Published by Jonquil Books, an imprint of Miglior Press

Jonquil Books
P. O. Box 7487
Athens, Georgia 30604

www.migliorpress.com

Calligraphy by Kenneth Williams

Printed in the United States of America

ISBN 978-0-9827614-0-3

10 9 8 7 6 5 4 3 2 1

First Edition

This book is written to honor the poetry
that lives in youthful hearts of people of all ages.
It is dedicated to children and grandchildren everywhere,
especially Daphne, Vivi, Brock, and Mac.

❧

"Poetry is the language in which [we explore our] own amazement."
—Christopher Fry

"Like butterflies in spring, poetry awakens the spirit,
stirs the imagination, and explores the possibilities
with each stroke of its rhythmic wings."
—Jamie Lynn Morris

Come join us as we celebrate a whole year in poems!

Spring and summer, fall and winter.

Robins and bluebirds and humming-birds.

Holidays and ordinary days.

Butterflies and rainbows and snowballs.

All these and more are waiting for you
in our new book of poems.

Let's go!

A SPRING WALK

We walked beside a field today
And took our time along the way.
The field was green with new-grown hay,
And bees and crickets were at play.
By the creek near woodland shade,
Flowers bloomed in a tiny glade.

We stopped to take a moment's rest,
Smiled at a sparrow's puffed-up chest,
In brave defense of her fledglings' nest
From uninvited human guests.
We watched the flowers, one by one,
As each bloom opened to the sun.

We saw a butterfly, poised and still,
Atop a yellow daffodil.
And as we watched it flutter by,
It seemed that we had wings to fly.

SPRINGTIME TREASURES

I awoke today before the sun.
I could not stay in bed asleep.
Springtime's pleasures had begun.
I jumped up with a happy leap.

Bird songs ring from fields and skies,
"Welcome, welcome new sunrise!"
Their notes float on a gentle breeze
Perfumed by violets and trees.

This morning's treasure trove, moreover,
Holds priceless jewels I can reap—
Diamonds clustered in the clover,
Winking in a sunlit sweep.
Joyfully, I look them over,
Then place them in my heart to keep.

TO A ROBIN

Robin, with the rust-red breast,
Puff the feathers on your chest.

Your arrival on the lawn,
Coinciding with the dawn,
Made you first to catch a worm
Before to safety it could squirm.

Now you can face the morning sky
And sing, "What an early bird am I!"

To A Bluebird

Bluebird, you took the color of the sky
In which you fly.

Now on a fence post you sit and sing,
And with your songs
The meadows stir and forests ring—
Your cheerful call announcing spring.

HUMMINGBIRDS

Hummingbirds, you dart-about things,
With fluttering, spinning, unseen wings!

You work so hard to stay in the air,
Seeking nectar your constant care.

It seems unfair in nature's scheme
You have so little time to dream.

I MEANT TO DRIVE TO WORK TODAY

I meant to drive to work today.
I was up at dawn to join the fray.
The city with its office towers
Required me for at least eight hours.

But a bird song beckoned me to stay,
And since I was early anyway,
A few more minutes could do no harm
To watch the sunrise o'er the farm.

I knew I should be leaving soon,
But circling swallows kept me 'til noon.
Then red-winged blackbirds seemed to chatter,
"Another hour could hardly matter."

By afternoon I couldn't part
From nature's feathered works of art,
As crimson cardinals and purple martins
Chirped, "Now's no time to be departing!"

As shadows grew long, I thought of town,
But a dazzling sunset held me bound
By its stunning skyworks' light revival,
As a whippoorwill hailed night's arrival.

I might have gone to work today.
I could have earned my daily pay.
But nature's treasures made me stay—
And a beckoning bird song got in my way.

THE EASTER BUNNY

He seems to us so funny,
That busy Easter bunny,
With big ears and puffy tail,
Bouncing along his bunny trail.

Although we've never seen him
(and would rather see than be him),
We thank that silly rabbit
For keeping true his habit:

Each Easter before dawn,
Hop-hopping across our lawn,
He leaves baskets full of treasures—
Colored eggs and chocolate pleasures—
That fill our eager tummies
With happy springtime yummies!

THE LAST DAY OF SCHOOL

We passed our test. Hooray! Hooray!
Let's celebrate the last school day.
School was good, our lessons learned,
Vacation time we now have earned.

Look! There's Flip waiting for us.
Wave 'bye to schoolmates on the bus.
We'll see them soon for games and fun
On days blessed by the summer sun.

SUMMER VACATION

What fills our hearts with great elation?
Why, every day of summer vacation!

We wake up early, and when chores are done,
We run outside for summer fun.

Let's build a fort or take a hike,
Check the garden or ride a bike,

Visit friends and play a game —
No two days will be the same!

When twilight comes and shadows grow,
We watch the flickering fireflies glow.

Each night tucked in our comfy beds,
Happy memories fill our heads.

FLIP'S NEW FRIEND

More schoolmates came to visit today
With lots of ideas for games to play.
They brought with them (this is the truth)
Their new French poodle, whose name is Ruth.

Flip acted timid, even shy,
When this strange dog came prancing by.
Did he want to growl, give Ruth a scare,
Pretty Ruth with a bow in her hair?
No! Flip barked and began to run.
Ruth gave chase, both having fun.

They chased each other, unafraid,
Then stopped to rest in a spot of shade.
They had run a race both dogs would win,
For each had found a brand new friend!

INDEPENDENCE DAY

In 1776 –
No king's cruel laws from across the sea
Could stop the sweep of democracy
And the liberty for which it stands
From taking hold throughout our land.

From the original thirteen colonies
There came a Declaration
Of Independence for our nation.
Now we're the fifty United States
That each American celebrates.

So rejoice and let the fireworks fly
For America's birthday, the Fourth of July!

DAYDREAMING ON A SUMMER DAY

Just like birds or butterflies
Gliding on a summer breeze,
You and I can tour the skies
Over towns and fields and trees.

As the clouds go floating by,
We'll sing a song of mirth,
Then find a rainbow in the sky
And slide on it to earth.

Nothing is impossible—
Or so to us it seems —
On wings of the imaginings
That make up our daydreams.

BACK TO SCHOOL

It's summer's end, vacation's done,
Our easy, carefree days are gone.

But back to school can be such fun!
We'll meet new friends, and teachers, too.
Our pencils, textbooks, all are new.

Here we climb aboard the bus
With new adventures ahead of us!

OCTOBER

Crown jewel of the autumn season,
If for no other single reason,
Your cloudless sky's brilliant hue
Best defines the color blue.

You soften summer's sultry end
With your invigorating blend
Of frosty nights and sunny days,
As birds fly south in migrant ways.

But you give us so much more,
As each bright dawn reveals its score
Of reds and golds of falling leaves,
Which paint our landscape with each breeze.

As bursting seedpods fill the air
With tiny wisps of windswept hair,
Mother Nature enjoys her fling
Before she sleeps and dreams of spring.

ONE MORE HOUR TODAY

As I gaze into the afternoon,
I find daylight ending much too soon.
The brisk, clean feel of shortened days
Foretells that winter's cold, damp ways
Will soon descend upon the Earth
And blow away our summer mirth.

Oh, Nature, use your magic power!
Extend this day another hour.
And if you grant me this repose,
Allow me one more scent of rose,
While your crystal blue autumn skies
Reflect the wonder in my eyes.

HALLOWEEN

We're all dressed up for Halloween,
The daring pirate and the royal queen.

Let ghosts and goblins come our way.
We're not afraid. We'll save the day!

Come, Flip, let's go trick or treating.
But wait!
Who spoke that spooky greeting?

Who said, "Who?"
Not us.
Was it you?

A THANKSGIVING PRAYER

We bow our heads and humbly pray
To give thanks on this special day,
For the gift of life, the gift of love,
For a bountiful harvest, for stars above,
For a warming sun, a quenching rain,
For dear old friends, and those we'll gain.

Lord, guide us through this coming year.
Keep us safe and free from fear.
Show us how each day to share
With those in need of help or care.

GETTING READY FOR CHRISTMAS

What fills our hearts with joy and glee?
Why, decorating the Christmas tree!
With crackling fire, the family near,
The evening's filled with warmth and cheer.

We've hung our stockings for Santa Claus—
Look! Flip has ribbon on his paws!
Did he unwrap a Christmas treat,
Thinking it was time to eat?

KEEPING WATCH FOR SANTA

It's Christmas Eve, the lights shine bright,
So Santa will find our house tonight.

It would be fun to stay up all night
To watch for Santa—he'd be a sight!

But Mom and Dad say we must sleep
So our Christmas wishes Santa will keep.

So it's off to bed, but while we dream,
We'll see Santa and his reindeer team,
Sailing along the Milky Way,
With toys we'll find on Christmas Day.

DID FLIP SEE SANTA?

At midnight our Yuletide home was still.
Outside, snow sparkled in the winter chill.

Was there a noise only Flip could hear?
Perhaps the crunch of a sleigh landing near?

Did Flip slip downstairs on silent paws
To share a treat with Santa Claus?

Did he see Santa this Christmas Eve?
He won't say, but we believe!

WINTER FUN

Snow is falling, soft and light.
It may throughout this wintry night.
Tomorrow we'll have snowy fun
Before it's melted by the sun.

We'll bundle up, wear our mittens,
So we won't get ourselves frostbitten.
We'll build a snowman, round and white,
Then have a great big snowball fight!

We'll pull our sleds way up the hill,
Then slide down fast without a spill.
But if we get cold or start to tire,
We'll drink hot chocolate by the fire.

PROMISES OF SPRING

As earth sleeps in winter's chill,
Silent flakes fly across the sky,
And snow grows on our windowsill.

Beside the glowing hearth we sigh
And listen to the fire sing
Its happy promises of spring.

THE
END

WORD LIST

Bee

Bluebird

Butterfly

Cardinal

Cat

Christmas Tree

WORD LIST

Cricket

Daffodil

Fireplace

Hummingbird

Mittens

Mouse

WORD LIST

Nest

Owl

Pencils

Pumpkin

Rabbit

Rainbow

WORD LIST

Ribbon

Robin

School Bus

Sunflower

Textbooks

Turkey

For Kathy, my best of everything.

—Grady Thrasher
August 2010